In the Footsteps of Explorers

Antoine
de La Mothe
Cadillac

French settlements at Detroit and Louisiana

Anders Knudsen

Crabtree Publishing Company

www.crabtreebooks.com

Crabtree Publishing Company

www.crabtreebooks.com

Til mine bedsteforældre

Coordinating editor: Ellen Rodger
Series editor: Carrie Gleason
Project editor: L. Michelle Nielsen
Editors: Rachel Eagen, Adrianna Morganelli
Design and production coordinator: Rosie Gowsell
Cover design and production assistance: Samara Parent
Art direction: Rob MacGregor
Scanning technician: Arlene Arch-Wilson
Photo research: Allison Napier

Consultant: Dr. Dennis Zembala, Director, Detroit Historical Museums

Photo Credits: Peabody Essex Museum, Salem, Massachusetts, USA/ The Bridgeman Art Library International: p. 5 (top right), p. 13 (top right), p. 27 (top right), p. 29 (top right); Private Collection/ The Bridgeman Art Library International: p. 26; Courtesy of the Burton Historical Collection, Detroit Public Library: p. 14, p. 15; W. Cody/ Corbis: p. 18; Reinhard Eisele/ Corbis: pp. 16-17; Owen Franken/ Corbis: p. 27 (top left); James Randklev/ Corbis: pp. 30-31; G.E. Kidder Smith/ Corbis: p. 10; The Granger Collection, New York: cover, p. 9, p. 11, p. 13 (left), p. 17, p. 19, p. 21, p. 24 (both); Shelia Broumley/ istock International: p. 5 (bottom left);Y Hui/ istock International: p. 5 (bottom right); Mike Morley/ istock International: pp. 20-21; North Wind/ Nancy Carter/ North Wind Picture Archives: p. 23; North Wind/ North Wind Picture Archives: p. 6, p. 7, p. 8, p. 22, p. 25, p. 28, p. 29 (top left); www.ronkimball.com: p. 30 (both). Other images from stock photo cd.

Illustrations: Adrianna Morganelli: p. 4; Lauren Fast, p. 7

Cartography: Jim Chernishenko: title page, p. 12

Cover: Cadillac had 100 men with him when he first landed at the site where Fort Pontchartrain du Détroit would be built.

Title page: Cadillac traveled great distances over the course of his career, often by boat. Sailing from Europe to the New World meant first traveling south to meet the trade winds, a westerly wind that blows from the north of Africa to the south of North America, making the voyage faster and easier.

Sidebar icon: Native Americans smoked tobacco to cure illnesses, and during spiritual ceremonies and peace agreements. Each Native group used different materials to make and decorate their pipes, such as wood, stone, clay, antlers, and feathers.

Library and Archives Canada Cataloguing in Publication

Knudsen, Anders
    Antoine de La Mothe Cadillac : French settlements at Detroit and Louisiana / Anders Knusen.

(In the footsteps of explorers)
Includes index.
ISBN-13: 978-0-7787-2429-2 (bound)
ISBN-10: 0-7787-2429-8 (bound)
ISBN-13: 978-0-7787-2465-0 (pbk)
ISBN-10: 0-7787-2465-4 (pbk)

    1. Cadillac, Antoine Laumet de Lamothe, 1658-1730--Juvenile literature. 2. Explorers--New France--Biography--Juvenile literature. 3. Frontier and pioneer life--New France--Juvenile literature. 4. Governors--Louisiana--Biography--Juvenile literature. 5. Detroit (Mich.)--History--Juvenile literature. 6. Detroit (Mich.)--Biography--Juvenile literature. 7. Canada--History--To 1763 (New France)--Juvenile literature. 8. Louisiana--History--To 1803--Juvenile literature. 9. France--Colonies--America--Juvenile literature. I. Title. II. Series.

F574.D453C35 2006   j977.4'3401092   C2006-902142-2

Library of Congress Cataloging-in-Publication Data

Knudsen, Anders.
    Antoine de la Mothe Cadillac : French settlements at Detroit and Louisiana / written by Anders Knudsen.
        p. cm. -- (In the footsteps of explorers)
    Includes index.
    ISBN-13: 978-0-7787-2429-2 (rlb)
    ISBN-10: 0-7787-2429-8 (rlb)
    ISBN-13: 978-0-7787-2465-0 (pbk)
    ISBN-10: 0-7787-2465-4 (pbk)
    1. Cadillac, Antoine Laumet de Lamothe, 1658-1730--Juvenile literature. 2. Detroit (Mich.)--History--Juvenile literature. 3. Detroit (Mich.)--Biography--Juvenile literature. 4. Explorers--New France--Biography--Juvenile literature. 5. Frontier and pioneer life--New France--Juvenile literature. 6. Canada--History--To 1763 (New France)--Juvenile literature. 7. Louisiana--History--To 1803--Juvenile literature. 8. Governors--Louisiana--Biography--Juvenile literature. 9. France--Colonies--America--Juvenile literature. I. Title. II. Series.
    F574.D453C33155 2006
    977.4'3401092--dc22
    [B]   2006012400

Crabtree Publishing Company

Published in Canada
Crabtree Publishing
616 Welland Ave.
St. Catharines, Ontario
L2M 5V6

Published in the
United States
Crabtree Publishing
PMB16A
350 Fifth Ave., Suite 3308
New York, NY 10118

Published in the
United Kingdom
Crabtree Publishing
White Cross Mills
High Town, Lancaster
LA1 4XS

Published in Australia
Crabtree Publishing
386 Mt. Alexander Rd.
Ascot Vale (Melbourne)
VIC 3032

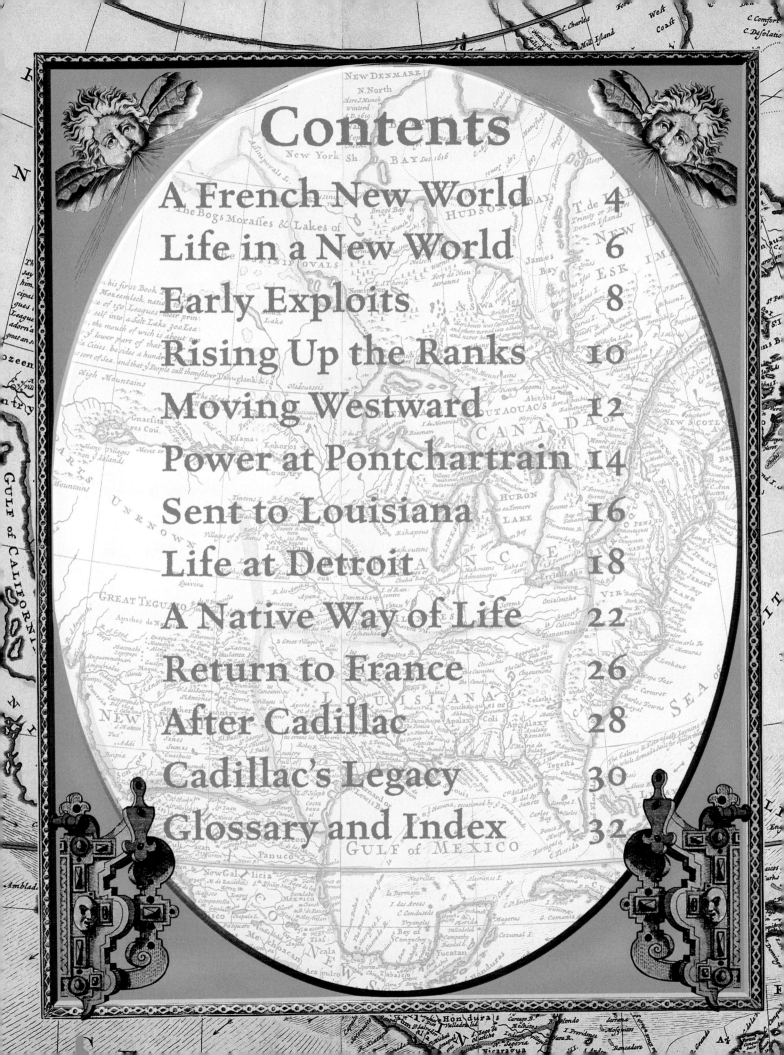

Contents

A French New World

Antoine de La Mothe Cadillac was a French adventurer who founded Detroit, and governed the territory of Louisiana. He convinced settlers to move to these isolated places, hoping to build settlements that could defend New France from enemies.

New France

New France was the name of lands in North America that were ruled by France. In Cadillac's lifetime, New France included territory in the present-day province of Nova Scotia, Canada, as well as the St. Lawrence Valley, the Great Lakes region, and the Mississippi Valley as far south as the Gulf of Mexico. The French king was interested in these lands because they were rich with valuable resources, including metal and mineral **deposits**, as well as fur-bearing animals. These goods would then be sent back to France and sold.

Taking the West

The French wanted to expand their territory further west. The English had already claimed territory south of the St. Lawrence Valley, as far as present-day Georgia, and were also looking to claim more territory in the west. Cadillac planned to build a settlement at a site on the **strait** between Lake Erie and Lake Huron. He wanted to build a fort and create **alliances** with Native groups. He hoped this would stop the English from moving into the Great Lakes region. This settlement was called "Detroit," after the French word for "strait."

(above) Cadillac liked to be in charge. He often squabbled, or argued, with other officials, including his superiors.

In the Words of...

Cadillac founded the Detroit settlement in 1701. He sent letters praising the site to **government officials** in France and Quebec, a major settlement in New France located at present-day Quebec City, in Canada. Cadillac believed that a strong settlement of French colonists, soldiers, and Native allies would be safe from attack by their enemies, which included the English and Haudenosaunee, also known as the Iroquois.

"This river or strait of the seas is scattered over, from one lake to the other...with large clusters of trees surrounded by charming meadows;...On the banks and round about the clusters of timber there is an infinite number of fruit trees... They are so well laid out that they might be taken for orchards planted by the hand of a gardener...I shall ever maintain that, if this post is settled by Frenchmen...it will be the safeguard of our trade with our allies, and the blow which will overpower the Iroquois,...because in consequence of it he will not be in a position to begin or to maintain war."

~ Antoine de La Mothe Cadillac

In Cadillac's letters, he wrote of the many plum and apple trees at Detroit.

- 1658 -
Cadillac is born in St. Nicolas de la Grave, France.

- 1683 -
Cadillac arrives in Acadia, a French settlement in present-day Nova Scotia, Canada.

- 1701 -
Cadillac founds Fort Pontchartrain du Détroit.

- 1730 -
Cadillac dies at his home in France.

Life in a New World

The French founded colonies in the New World so they could send furs and other resources back to France. Many men who came to New France hoped to grow rich by trading furs, while others came to escape poverty. Settlements grew, and many workers were needed, including farmers and builders.

Merchant Companies

Most of the money earned in New France came from **exporting** furs back to France. The king of France granted groups of merchants who came together as companies a monopoly, or sole control, of the fur trade in a specific area. Merchant companies earned high **profits** selling New World furs in France. Merchant companies were also often given control of new settlements. On top of managing trade, they had to pay for the people and materials needed to build the settlement. This saved the French government money, while still expanding French territory in North America.

The Beaver Hat

The most valuable fur was the beaver pelt. In France, beaver fur was used to make felt hats. The felt, which was made from the softest fur of the beaver pelt, was admired in France for its beauty. Beaver hats were expensive and it was a sign of wealth and **status** to own one.

Native groups hunted beaver and other fur-bearing animals. They traded the furs with the French, in exchange for metal goods and guns.

The Threat to the South

To the south of New France were the English territories of New England and New York. English settlers traded with the local Native peoples along the Hudson and Mohawk rivers. The English wanted control over the fur trade and tried to convince Native groups, who were allied with the French, to trade with them. The English were also eager to expand their lands into the Great Lakes region, which was French territory.

Native Allies

Since the founding of New France, the French had been enemies of the Haudenosaunee, a confederacy, or group, of five Native nations. French colonists befriended the Huron, or Wendat, the Odawa, and other groups that were enemies of the Haudenosaunee. The English allied with the Haudenosaunee in the hopes that they would help defeat the French.

(background) Coureurs de bois, or "runners of the woods," were French traders who learned how to travel and hunt from Native peoples.

- 1534 -
Jacques Cartier (above) is the first to claim lands in North America for France.

- 1608 -
French explorer Samuel de Champlain founds a settlement at present-day Quebec City.

- 1682 -
Rene Cavalier, Sieur de La Salle, takes control of lands around the Mississippi River for France and names the region Louisiana.

Early Exploits

Cadillac was born Antoine Laumet. His father, a judge, made sure his son had a good education. Cadillac dreamed of being a rich noble, a person with a high rank in society.

Lying for a New Life

As a young man, Cadillac was a low-ranking **cadet** in the French army. At the age of 25, he sailed across the Atlantic, landing at the French settlement of Port Royal in present-day Nova Scotia. Cadillac told the other settlers that he was a noble and changed his name to Antoine de La Mothe Cadillac, which sounded like the name of a nobleman. He also lied about his rank in the army, claiming he had been a **lieutenant**.

A Privateer's Apprentice

In Port Royal, Cadillac joined the ship of a privateer, François Guyon. Privateers were legal pirates hired by the government to capture ships of another country and take the cargo onboard. Cadillac's experience sailing with Guyon helped him build the skills needed to become a **navigator**. In 1687, Cadillac married Marie-Thérèse Guyon, François Guyon's niece. Guyon gave the couple a plot of land in Acadia as a gift.

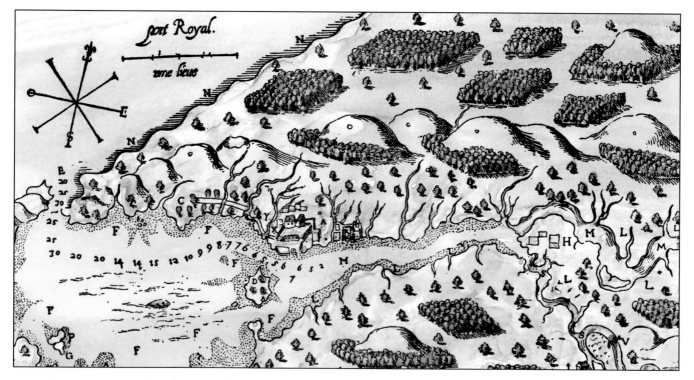

Port Royal was in Acadia, a colony that included parts of present-day Nova Scotia and Maine.

Struggles in Acadia

Cadillac wanted to trade with the Native peoples who lived near Port Royal. He formed a trading partnership with two government officials who worked at Port Royal. The governor of Acadia opposed the partnership because officials were not allowed to trade. Cadillac tried to get the governor fired by encouraging settlers and soldiers to disobey his orders. His plan backfired when King Louis XIV of France learned that Cadillac was trying to **sabotage** the governor. The king broke up the partnership. Cadillac was forced to put his plans for wealth on hold.

War with the English

In 1689, war broke out between the English and French. At Port Royal, Cadillac was placed in charge of building stronger **fortifications**. He was then hired by Louis de Baude de Frontenac, the governor of New France, to make maps of the New England and New York coastlines, which the French could use to attack the English. While Cadillac was away, an English **fleet** landed at Port Royal. English soldiers captured the fort and burned several buildings. Cadillac's home was destroyed.

(background) Control over Acadia went back and forth between the English and French. Many French settlers, called Acadians, stayed after the English took over. The Acadian Expulsion began in 1755 and involved the English removing Acadians from their homes by force.

Rising Up the Ranks

After losing his home in Port Royal, Cadillac and his family sailed to the Quebec settlement. Governor Frontenac made Cadillac a lieutenant and sent him on an expedition to map the New England coast. When Cadillac returned he was promoted to captain.

Sent to the West

In 1694, Cadillac was given command of Michilimackinac, the French fort at the straits connecting Lake Michigan and Lake Huron. Michilimackinac was largely inhabited by soldiers and traders, and was located in the middle of lands held by Native allies, including the Odawa and the Wendat. Cadillac's job was to manage trade with the local Native peoples, keep peaceful relations with them, and convince them to fight against the Haudenosaunee.

Native Peoples at Michilimackinac

Unfortunately for Cadillac, the Native groups around Michilimackinac were not willing to follow the French into war. They did not believe the French could protect them against the Haudenosaunee. While Cadillac succeeded in keeping the Native allies friendly with the French, he could not stop them from making peace with the Haudenosaunee or the English.

Fort Michilimackinac was protected by soldiers who kept watch during the day and night.

Fur and Brandy

While commander of Michilimackinac, Cadillac made a lot of money selling goods, especially brandy, an alcoholic drink made by the French. Even though officers were not supposed to trade, the king allowed it at Michilimackinac to help maintain friendly relations with the local Native peoples. Cadillac also made money by **seizing** the furs of the *coureurs de bois*. To get their furs back, the *coureurs de bois* were forced to pay the high prices Cadillac charged. In 1697, the French king temporarily stopped the beaver trade. Too many pelts had been shipped to Europe, which meant furs were easy to come by, prices were falling, and traders were losing money. All those at western trade posts were forced to leave. Cadillac returned to Quebec.

(background) *Jesuit missionaries were sent to North America to preach Catholicism to the local Native peoples. The Jesuits did not like that brandy was traded at Michilimackinac.*

Moving Westward

In 1698, Cadillac sailed for France to present a plan for a new settlement in the Great Lakes region. He wanted to build a fort where French settlers and Native peoples lived as neighbors. Cadillac wanted French soldiers to live among the settlers to protect them from the English, who wanted to claim the region for themselves.

Quebec •

Port Royal •

Montreal •

Lake Superior

Fort Michilimackinac •

Lake Huron

Lake Ontario

Lake Michigan

Fort Pontchartrain du Détroit

Lake Erie

Cadillac's route to Detroit in 1701: ➤➤➤

Cadillac's route to Louisiana in 1713: ➤➤➤

Fort Saint Louis •

The Plan for Detroit

In France, Cadillac presented his plan to Jerome Phelypeaux de Pontchartrain, the king's official who was in charge of colonies. Cadillac planned to build a fort on the river connecting Lake Erie and Lake Huron, now called the Detroit River. Native peoples would be given land close to the fort to settle and would be encouraged to learn the French language and ways of life, making them closer allies. Cadillac's plan was approved.

Setting Out

In 1701, Cadillac prepared his expedition. He recruited 100 men, purchased boats, as well as three months' worth of food and supplies. They took a long, indirect route because the quicker path through Lake Ontario and Lake Erie went through Haudenosaunee lands. After reaching the Detroit River, they chose a site that would be easy to defend, and started building the fort. Cadillac named the settlement Fort Pontchartrain du Détroit.

French Women at Detroit

Cadillac's wife, Marie-Thérèse, arrived at Detroit in early 1702 with a group of settlers, including one other woman. The French and Haudenosaunee had made peace in the summer of 1701, allowing the group to take the shorter route through Haudenosaunee lands. The arrival of French women was important, because it proved that Cadillac's goal was to make Detroit a permanent settlement. By 1707, over 270 settlers lived at Detroit.

In early 1702, two of Cadillac's five children were living at Detroit.

- July 1701 -
Cadillac arrives at Detroit.

- August 4, 1701 -
A peace treaty is signed creating a temporary peace between the French and Haudenosaunee.

- 1704 -
Cadillac's daughter is the first French child born at Detroit.

- May 1710 -
Cadillac is removed from his position as governor of Detroit.

Power at Pontchartrain

In the fall of 1701, the French crown granted control of Detroit to a merchant company called the Company of the Colony. Cadillac was disappointed because he believed he would be in control of Detroit.

Fighting for Control

The Company of the Colony sent **clerks** to Detroit to manage the fur trade. Cadillac wrote letters to the king's official, Pontchartrain, attacking the Company of the Colony. He claimed they were taking higher profits from the trade than allowed by the king. He also reported successes he had achieved at Detroit, such as convincing 6,000 Native peoples to settle in the area. Cadillac's reports, along with a letter of praise sent by the governor of Montreal, convinced Pontchartrain to side with Cadillac. In 1705, the king gave control of Detroit to Cadillac.

(above) Most settlers at Detroit lived within the walls of the fort. Outside the walls, farmers planted crops and many Native groups set up villages.

The *Le Pesant* Affair

The Odawa, Miami, and other Native groups had moved their villages close to Detroit. Cadillac promised to act as judge in conflicts between the groups. In 1706, a war chief of the Odawa, who the French called *Le Pesant*, thought that the Miami were going to attack his village. He led a group of warriors in an attack against the Miami. Five Miami chiefs, a French priest, and a French soldier were killed. The French captured *Le Pesant*, but Cadillac did not put him to death, as the Miami demanded. Feeling betrayed, the Miami attacked the French, killing three men.

Under Investigation

After hearing news of the battles in Detroit, Pontchartrain hired an official to investigate the way Cadillac was running Detroit. The official found the colony in very poor condition, describing it as much smaller and less populated than Cadillac had described in his letters. He also learned that the Native peoples near Detroit had made peace with the Haudenosaunee, and had begun trading with the English. After reading this report, Pontchartrain decided to remove Cadillac from his position in Detroit.

(background) St. Anne's Church was the first building at Detroit. A church with the same name still exists in Detroit today.

Sent to Louisiana

Despite Cadillac's failure at Detroit, Pontchartrain made him the governor of Louisiana in 1710. Cadillac's job was to strengthen the forts within the colony, build up trade, and stop the English from moving into the west. Cadillac was not happy with his position.

Financial Support

After losing his position at Detroit, Cadillac returned to France. His first task was to find someone to finance, or provide money, to run the colony. He wrote to Antoine Crozat, a wealthy businessman, boasting of Louisiana as a colony rich with mines of gold and silver waiting to be found. Crozat agreed to finance the colony. He formed the Company of Louisiana, and sent a representative, Jean-Baptiste Duclos, to Louisiana to oversee, or watch over, how his money would be spent.

A Struggling Colony

Cadillac and his family arrived at Fort Saint Louis, the main French settlement in Louisiana, in 1713. The settlement was in poor condition. Food supplies sent from France were rotting in the warm climate. More settlers were needed to help build stronger forts, especially along the Mississippi River, to prevent the English from expanding into the west. Cadillac also needed settlers to grow products for trade, such as tobacco, and find mines rich with valuable metals, so the colony could survive. Cadillac was also in charge of forming alliances with Native groups, such as the Choctaw and Natchez peoples.

(background) Fort Saint Louis was built on Mobile Bay at present-day Mobile, Alabama. Much of the area around Mobile Bay was swamplands and marshes.

Making Enemies

Before Cadillac even arrived in Louisiana, he argued with Duclos over how to run the colony. Cadillac did not like sharing power, and soon after arriving in Louisiana he became an enemy of the highest-ranking military officer in the colony, Jean-Baptiste le Moyne, Sieur de Bienville. Cadillac charged Bienville with stealing food and supplies. The soldiers and officers in Louisiana were loyal to Bienville, who had been in command of the **garrison** at Fort Louis for ten years. The soldiers began refusing Cadillac's orders.

Failure

Settlers and soldiers in the colony grew angry at the high prices charged for supplies. Many began trading secretly with Spanish traders living in a nearby settlement in present-day Florida. This was illegal because all trade in the colony was to be overseen by Cadillac. The Natchez people, who supplied the French with deerskins, also began trading more with the Spanish and English because they could get better prices. In 1716, after hearing of Cadillac's poor leadership, Crozat stripped him of his position and ordered him back to France.

When Cadillac was governor, Louisiana stretched from present-day Minnesota in the north to the Gulf of Mexico in the south. At the time, the French only had a few forts along the Illinois and Mississippi rivers and some settlements along the Gulf of Mexico.

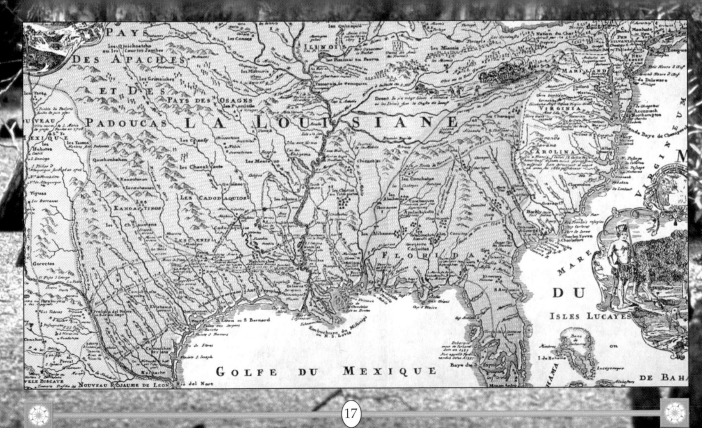

Life at Detroit

The first years in a new settlement were difficult. To survive, settlers had to adapt, or learn how to live in their new environment. In most cases, settlements were built near an ocean, lake, or river because transporting people and supplies was easier and faster by boat.

Building a Settlement

The first structure built at most settlements, including Detroit, was a palisade, or defensive wall. Palisades were built using wooden stakes that were sharpened at both ends and driven deep into the ground. Next, buildings such as warehouses to store supplies were constructed, and land was cleared and prepared for farming crops.

The Seigneurial System

Land in new settlements throughout New France was given to settlers using the seigneurial system. The crown gave land, or entire settlements, to seigneurs, or people of high rank. As commander of Detroit, Cadillac became a seigneur. He divided up the land at Detroit into plots, which were given to farmers and other settlers who had to pay a fee to Cadillac each year. If settlers left, their land was given back to Cadillac.

(background) Walls for houses were made using wooden stakes. Mud or mortar was used to fill in the spaces between the stakes. Mortar was made by mixing crushed limestone or seashells with water, and then adding clay, straw, or sand.

Within the Walls

Most settlers at Detroit, even farmers whose crops were outside the fort, lived within the palisade. The palisade and the soldiers living at the fort protected the settlers against attacks from enemies. Supplies, including some food, were shipped from the Montreal settlement but Cadillac did not want to rely on other settlements for help. Many settlers had small gardens where they grew food for their families. Barns were later built to house horses, oxen, and cattle, an important source of milk and meat.

Under Cadillac's Command

Nearly all decisions about the construction and running of Detroit had to be approved by Cadillac. Along with managing the fur trade at Detroit and acting as seigneur, Cadillac also acted as judge. He settled disputes and had the power to arrest and imprison settlers he felt were disrupting life at the settlement. Cadillac controlled Detroit but had to report to government officials in France and the governor of New France. The governor represented the king and controlled the military in the colony.

The warehouse Cadillac had built was made from boards cut at a saw mill. Detroit also had a wind-powered flour mill and a powder magazine, or a building used to store gunpowder.

Working the Land

In the early years at Detroit, settlers had to gather food in the forest, hunt, and trade for corn from Native peoples to survive. Farming was important to the survival of the settlers. By 1710, Cadillac had given more than 60 plots of land to farmers. The farms were long strips of land that were called ribbon farms. Each farm ended at the Detroit River, so the farmers could use the river to transport their crops, which included apples, wheat, and peas, back to the settlement.

Settlers grew crops introduced to them by Native peoples, such as corn and squash, as well as wheat, peas, and other crops that were traditionally grown in Europe.

Sagamité

Corn was one of the most important foods of the New World. Native peoples taught the French how to prepare corn. One popular corn dish was called sagamité, which is an Algonquian name for corn stew. Ask an adult to help you make sagamité.

Ingredients:
4 cups (1,000 mL) water
1 cup (250 mL) cornmeal
1 or 2, 6 to 8 ounce (170 to 227 gram) whitefish fillets
4 tablespoons (60 mL) butter

Directions:
1. In a soup pot, bring the water to a boil. Add the cornmeal, stir, then lower heat. Simmer for 20 minutes.
2. Heat the butter in a large frying pan. Fry the whitefish for two minutes on each side.
3. Flake the fish into the soup pot. Simmer for another 20 minutes.
4. Add other seasonings, such as salt and pepper, if you like.

The Church

The only man at Detroit who Cadillac did not have authority over was the priest, or leader of the **Roman Catholic** Church. The priest led **mass** for settlers and Native peoples he was trying to **convert**, treated the sick, and encouraged people to live religious and honest lives.

Spare Time

Settlers and soldiers came together in the evenings to dance, sing songs, and tell stories. They also enjoyed playing games, such as checkers and cards. Higher ranking officers, including Cadillac, often spent time fencing, or sword fighting.

Native peoples taught the French how to play lacrosse. Lacrosse is a game where a ball is thrown and caught using a long stick that has a net at one end. Two teams play, each trying to score on the other's goal.

A Native Way of Life

Each Native nation in North America had their own traditions and lifestyles. They also spoke dialects that were specific to where they lived. Most of the dialects spoken in the Great Lakes region belonged to either the Algonquian or Iroquoian language groups.

Clans to Confederacies

Native nations were often made up of family groupings, or clans, headed by chiefs. Chiefs were often chosen by the people, although some chiefs from nations in Louisiana inherited their positions. Many nations belonged to confederacies, or groups of nations that traded goods and helped protect each other against enemies. Confederacies brought together the chiefs from each nation to discuss issues, such as deciding to go to war against other nations.

Homes and Villages

Native groups that farmed lived in villages, where many families made their homes year-round. The Natchez people, as well as other Native groups from the southeast of Louisiana, built their homes using straw, grasses, and wood from trees that grew in the area. Some homes had walls that were built from woven saplings. The saplings were covered in plaster that was made from clay mixed with dry grass. Roofs were usually made of grass **thatch**.

The Haudenosaunee also lived in villages, but their homes were called longhouses. These wooden dwellings were usually about 100 feet (30 meters) long, and were covered in elm or cedar bark.

Mobile Homes

Native groups who depended on hunting and fishing rather than farming had to move between seasonal hunting grounds, so they needed temporary shelters. The Odawa of the Great Lakes laid animal skin mats over wooden frames to make wigwams, or oval-shaped tents. Since groups often returned to the same sites, the frames were left standing so they could be reused when the group returned.

(above) Many Native groups smoked tobacco at ceremonies. Peace pipes, or calumets, were smoked when peace was made between groups.

Native Inventions

Native peoples developed ways of traveling that made journeys easier. Many traveled over water in lightweight canoes made from birchbark. Canoes made from hollowed out tree trunks were made to carry heavy loads. In the north, snowshoes and toboggans were used when traveling over snowy terrain. To carry goods, women wove baskets from strips of wood or grass, and made bags from animal skins and corn husks. Many Native peoples also used animal skins to make clothing, moccasins, or shoes, and coverings for tents.

French Allies

The French promised their Native allies a fair price for furs as long as they were loyal to the French settlers. Many of their Native allies had been forced off their lands by the Haudenosaunee, and the French promised to fight with them against frequent attacks. The French in Louisiana gave guns, blankets, metal tools, and other gifts to local nations, such as the Choctaw, Chickasaw, and Natchez peoples to maintain alliances. The Chickasaw and Natchez nations sometimes switched their loyalties between the English, French, and Spanish, depending on who offered better prices for their furs.

European Arrival

Europeans came to North America in the 1600s and 1700s to seek riches and claim territory. When New France was founded in northeastern North America, some Native groups got along with the French, and traded furs for goods such as guns and iron tools, which were stronger than the tools they made from wood, stone, and animal bones. Other groups, including the Haudenosaunee, did not like the French because they took over their lands and helped their enemies.

(above) Wampum were bands of colorful beads. The designs represented historic events.

(right) Native Americans used wampum to tell stories about peace treaties and other events.

The Black Robes

In New France, missionaries from orders, or organized religious groups, such as the Jesuits and Récollects, hoped to convert Native peoples to Catholicism. Missionaries were sent to live with different Native groups, where they learned Native languages and performed religious services such as baptism, a ceremony where people were made members of the Church. Several Native nations called the Jesuits "Black Robes," after the black cloaks they wore.

The Impact of Disease

When Europeans came to North America, they brought with them many diseases, such as smallpox and influenza. The Native peoples of North America had never been exposed to these diseases and their bodies were not immune to them, or able to fight the diseases. Hundreds of thousands of Native peoples were killed by European diseases.

Native peoples believed that great spirits created the world, caused weather, and lived inside animals, trees, and rocks. Missionaries thought these beliefs were the devil's work.

Return to France

Cadillac returned to France in 1717. He was tired of traveling and felt his work at Detroit and Louisiana had not been rewarded enough to make further work in New France worthwhile.

Locked in the Bastille

When Cadillac and his family arrived in France, Cadillac was surprised to hear stories about Louisiana being a place of great riches. A new trading company was in charge of Louisiana and they were trying to encourage people to move there. Cadillac spoke out, telling people that the descriptions of Louisiana were not true. Cadillac was imprisoned for making speeches against the colonies.

Released

After four months in prison, Cadillac was released. Once out of jail, Cadillac went to the **court** to argue that he had not been paid enough for the years he had governed in Louisiana. He complained that he was completely broke. The court agreed to pay Cadillac a higher **salary**, and even awarded him the Cross of St. Louis, a medal to reward him for his service in New France.

Cadillac, and his son, Joseph, who was also arrested for speaking out against the colonies, was sent to the Bastille, a prison in Paris. The Bastille held many who were wrongly imprisoned by the king. It was stormed in 1789, marking the start of the French Revolution, a war that saw the king overthrown.

Cadillac became governor of Castelsarrasin, a region in France, after selling land granted to him in North America. Today, this region has many vineyards that produce grapes for winemaking.

Arguing His Case

Cadillac spent the next four years requesting greater rewards from the king for his work in New France. He argued he was owed for the success he had achieved at Detroit. Eventually, the king granted Cadillac a piece of land in Detroit, but it was not as large a piece as Cadillac wanted. The king also gave Cadillac ownership of some of the buildings he had constructed in Detroit.

Mayor of a Small Town

Cadillac quickly sold the lands and buildings he was granted in Detroit to a merchant in Paris. With the money, he bought the title of governor and mayor of a small town in France called Castelsarrasin, not far from St. Nicolas de la Grave. This position gave him a small annual salary. Cadillac lived quietly in St. Nicolas de la Grave with his family until his death in 1730.

- September 1717 -
Cadillac is imprisoned in Paris.

- 1722 -
Cadillac becomes governor and mayor of Castelsarrasin, a small town in France.

- 1730 -
Cadillac dies and is buried in Castelsarrasin.

After Cadillac

In the late 1600s and 1700s, four wars were fought in North America between the French and English, or British as they were known after uniting with Scotland in 1707. Both sides were looking to expand their territories. In 1763, the final war ended with New France losing most of its lands to the British.

Falling Behind in Trade

After each war, a peace treaty was signed but the French and British remained enemies. Both sides continued to build forts in the West and fought to control trade. The British offered Native peoples goods at cheap prices, and sent traders to urge Native groups, who were former allies of the French, to trade at their settlements. New France lost a great deal of its trade to the British.

Fighting Back

To keep their Native allies, the French built new trading forts close to Native communities and sent more traders to posts around the Great Lakes. They also lowered the prices of their goods. The French depended on Native alliances when they went to war against the British. The French and their Native allies won a number of battles against much larger British armies but the end of the final war saw New France defeated by the British.

The French and Indian War, fought from 1755 to 1763, was the last war fought between the French and British in North America. France and Great Britain were also at war in Europe.

After 1763, the British were the main power in present-day Canada and the United States. In 1783, American colonists defeated the British in the American Revolution, the war that formed the United States, and took over many British settlements, including Detroit.

Detroit after Cadillac

When Cadillac left Detroit, the fort began to fall apart and many settlers left. Not all of the Native peoples who lived close to the Detroit settlement got along with each other, and battles between groups often broke out. For the next 38 years, commanders at Detroit did little to improve the settlement and few new settlers arrived.

Into the Hands of the British

Detroit needed more settlers if it was going to survive future attacks by the British. New settlers began arriving in the early 1750s after the new commander of Detroit offered them land, farming tools, and other supplies. After New France was defeated in 1763, the colonists had no choice but to surrender Detroit to the British. The French settlers were allowed to keep their homes and land if they swore loyalty to the king of Great Britain.

- 1689 to 1697 -
The English capture Port Royal during King William's War. It is returned to the French when a peace treaty is signed.

- 1702 to 1713 -
The British fail to capture Quebec during Queen Anne's War. They get Acadia and other French lands in the peace agreement.

- 1744 to 1748 -
The British capture Louisburg, a French fort in present-day Nova Scotia, in King George's War.

Cadillac's Legacy

Cadillac's legacy can be seen in the areas he explored, especially Detroit. Detroit has grown into a major industrial city with streets, buildings, and a public square named in honor of Cadillac, and in acknowledgment of the city's French history.

The Cadillac

Antoine de La Mothe Cadillac is remembered for founding Detroit. In the early 1900s, Detroit became the center of the automobile industry in the United States. One of the earliest car companies was named after Cadillac. The company, owned by General Motors since 1909, became famous around the world for making luxury cars. The famous trademark of the car is based on Cadillac's coat of arms. A coat of arms was a symbol that represented a noble family's pride in their ancestry. They used it to decorate clothing and their homes.

Each Cadillac car, including this model from 1954, has Cadillac's coat of arms on its hood. Cadillac invented his coat of arms to make people believe he was a noble.

Cadillac's Legacy

Today, there are towns named after Cadillac in many of the regions that the adventurer explored, including the state of Michigan, the province of Quebec, Canada, and the southwest of France. A plaque in Mobile, Alabama, marks the home Cadillac lived in while he was governor of Louisiana and an entire museum is devoted to the explorer in Castelsarrasin, the village in France where he spent his final days.

French Remains

French communities can still be found in many areas of North America, the largest being the Canadian province of Quebec. Quebec, one of the original provinces of Canada, has a French culture, and French is the official language. Over 20,000 French-speaking people live in the province of Nova Scotia, many the descendants of Acadians. Cajun people in Louisiana descend from Acadians who were forced from their homes by the British during the Acadian Expulsion.

Cadillac and Marie-Thérèse were given land in present-day Maine as a wedding gift. Cadillac Mountain overlooks this parcel of land.

Glossary

adventurer A person who seeks out exciting experiences

alliance A partnership between peoples or countries

cadet Someone who is training to be in the military

captain A high ranked army officer who is often put in charge of other officers

Catholicism The religion of the Roman Catholic Church, an organization that is headed by the Pope

clerk Someone who is in charge of keeping records

colony Land ruled by a distant country

convert To change one's religion, faith, or beliefs

court A king and all those around him, including his family, personal servants, advisors, and officials

crown A king or queen that rules a country and its colonies

deposit A layer of valuable material that is found under the ground

devil The main evil spirit believed in by Catholics

dialect A language spoken by one group of people in a particular region

export To ship goods to be sold elsewhere for profit

fleet A group of ships or smaller boats

fortifications Structures, such as defensive walls, that protect a settlement

garrison A group of soldiers that protect a fort or settlement

govern To rule over people within a territory

government official A person who works on behalf of a governor or other ruler

Jesuit missionaries Members of a religious order called the Society of Jesus, who traveled to the New World to preach Catholicism to the Native peoples who lived there

language group A group of related languages or dialects

lieutenant Someone who acts on the behalf of someone with great power or authority

limestone A hard rock that is used to build structures

mass A religious celebration in the Roman Catholic Church

navigator Someone who is trained in methods of determining location

New World North, South, and Central America, including the Caribbean Islands

peace treaty An agreement between two or more peoples to stop fighting

profit The amount of money earned

rank A level of status or authority

Roman Catholic A Christian religion. The leader of the Roman Catholic Church is the Pope

sabotage To purposely make something bad happen

salary Regular payment of a fixed rate

seize To take something by legal right

status Being known in a community or society as having wealth and power

strait A narrow passage of water that connects two larger bodies of water

thatch A covering of grasses or other plant materials

Index

Printed in the U.S.A.